Treasure You Series
Book 1

Alignment

Treasure You Series

Book 1

Alignment

Reflections On Motherhood, Clarity, & Purpose

Dionna Rojas Orta

DEDICATION

This book is dedicated to the memory of
my grandmother **Elizabeth**. I miss you
every day, and we are sticking together.

ACKNOWLEDGEMENTS

To my "Unpluckables":

My Parents: **Donna & Martin**,
Mi Amigas: **Mayela & Ruth**
My Children and Grandchild: **Ashley,
Felipe Josue, Gabriel, Bryce**
My Sister: **Sherrae**
My Husband: **Phillip**

INTRODUCTION
Get In Alignment

In my early 20's I struggled with being a young, single mother in the body of Christ. I was conflicted. Most importantly I felt like I had let my parents, myself, and God down. One moment of rebellion in my eyes ended many dreams. "This life changing event could not have been in God's plans," I thought. "How can I accomplish my educational goals? Can I travel? How will I support the baby?"

I even aimed my frustration toward the Lord when I prayed, "Lord, how could you let me get pregnant when so many other girls my age have been intimate with people for years?" I know, the nerve of me, but who else could I blame? Blame and loss of hope plagued the early years of becoming a mother until I forgave myself for compromising my dreams and values.

The Aha moment came when I was taking my daughter to her first day of kindergarten. It hit me like a ton of bricks that I was responsible for this little person. My thought was, "Girl get it together, you're a mother and she needs you." I pulled up my big girl pants up that day and had a long talk with the Lord on my way to work. I had to forgive the young girl who got pregnant unexpectedly in order to stop living in the past. I chose to embrace the gift I had been given: "Motherhood." I have 31+ years of experience on my motherhood journey that include challenges, miracles, love, and victories.

As I matured in my walk with Christ, I realized that a sense of peace and balance in my roles seemed unachievable. As moms, we often find ourselves immersed in our roles, pursuing our passions, and working towards impactful goals. My family expanded from two to five in a five year time span. Peace and balance appeared to be unreachable and unrealistic for such a full and busy house until God highlighted how I viewed peace and balanced. It was an individualistic way of thinking. As a working mother and wife, I craved balance, but needed alignment. I was following Christ and serving Him, but when I was out of alignment, I felt unprepared, out of sync, and unsure.

Alignment requires a level of faith in God that will renew your mindset. You will go from "How can I achieve balance in my life and home?" To asking, "God what is my assignment today? How do you want me to serve? Who do you need me to work with or assist?

I hope this book of reflections will help you think about whether you are in alignment with God. As you read the reflections, ponder the questions and pray the prayers, my hope and prayer is that

you will find yourself coming into
agreement with God's plan.

Dionna

Father God,

I pray for each mother that finds herself reading this book. Father God I pray that as she reads through the pages of this devotional she will find aha moments and know she is not alone on her journey. Keep my sister safe emotionally, physically, and spiritually as she navigates her own motherhood journey. Renew her mind daily and help her to keep your word close to her heart.

Amen

Alignment

*An arrangement of groups
or forces related to one another.*

*The act of aligning,
or the state of being aligned.*

~Webster's Dictionary

Alignment

Contents

"Alignment requires a level of faith in God that will renew your mindset."

~Dionna Rojas

MASTER THE ART OF BALANCE

Many are the plans in a person's heart, but it is the LORD's purpose that prevails

Proverbs 19:21

Early in my career, I managed a family visitation program. The son of one of the parents in my program knocked on my office door one evening before his family arrived for a scheduled visit. He asked me, "Why do you seem to be the only person at the office all the time?"

His candid question left me momentarily puzzled. I tried to justify my actions, "I am committed to my job and to you. I want to ensure that you can reunite with your father."

He followed up with another question, "When do you see your own family?" That question struck a chord of clarity in me; I realized he had a valid point. My dedication to reuniting families became all-encompassing and I failed to recognize the subtle misalignment in my professional and personal priorities.

As I cleaned the visitation room after the visit, the young man's questions lingered in my mind. His concern was a wake-up call for me and a hard realization that my passion for helping others had encroached upon my commitment to be present for, and serve my family. It was time to reassess and set boundaries that would safeguard the delicate equilibrium between my professional and personal life.

Setting boundaries does not merely help you balance values and priorities; it is a tool that ensures your priorities stay aligned. It requires introspection, self-awareness, and courage to say no as you need to.

When you set boundaries, reflect on your priorities. Pay attention to warning signs indicating potential misalignment to the Holy Spirit's guidance. Are you neglecting family commitments for professional pursuits? What matters most to your values you live by?

Try not to set boundaries with a dusty lens. Here is the interesting thing about dust, it does not accumulate all at once. It can take days before you recognize that there is a film of dust on a surface. The same is true when we fall out of alignment with the priorities God has assigned to us.

It is not always a jarring drop of responsibilities, most times it can be compromises made when scheduling our days for something that seems important in the moment but not necessarily a priority. That is what happened to me on that fateful night at work. I was alerted in that conversation that I had been giving space to doing what I thought was right.

Like the sun ray exposing the dust coming through my dining room window I was able to examine the accumulation of good intentions and misalignment of priorities all at once. I did not like what I saw, and was immediately convicted about not consulting the Lord about how I was to support and help families. Simply put, my husband and children needed me too. The book of Proverbs has one of my favorite scriptures that I have learned to lean into since, "Trust in the Lord with all your heart and lean not unto your own understanding; in all your ways acknowledge Him and He will make your path straight, 3:5-6 (NIV).

This scripture has served as a reminder for me to trust that God knows best. As a mother I want to encourage you to remember that God is with you and understands your responsibilities at work and home. Acknowledging where you need God's guidance is the first step to aligning your plans to God's plan. This will help you set and communicate your boundaries clearly to colleagues, supervisors, and family members when you understand who you are representing in professional spaces and as a mother. This ensures mutual understanding and respect for your commitments in family life as well as business.

Lord,

Help me set boundaries. Transform my approach to both my professional and personal life. Allow me to be present for my family without compromising my dedication to helping others.

Amen

What matters most to me?

LOVE YOUR LOVED ONES WELL

"With all humility and gentleness, with patience, bearing with one another in love"

Ephesians 4:2 (ESV)

It is not always easy to know how to love and be loved by others. Do you ever feel that you are doing too much for someone or that you are not appreciated? You may find yourself asking if you are getting enough love in your life. According to Psychology Today[1], a five to 20 second hug has many benefits. It can affirm your love and value.

Incorporating self-care into your routine the same as you dedicate time to

---

[1] https://www.psychologytoday.com/us/blog/the-path-passionate-happiness/202203/the-shocking-truth-about-hugs

professional tasks and allocate time for personal well-being. This could be as simple as spending quality time with family or engaging in rejuvenating activities. If you create dedicated spaces for work and personal life you can stay focused on maintaining a healthy balance.

At times I felt ugly on the inside. I struggled to believe I was worth love, and I was insecure about affection. It didn't matter how much my sister, or if others complemented me on what they saw in me as a mother, I saw where I was falling short. I thought about how my children and husband couldn't possibly love me. I was so focused on myself that I failed to remember God's grace is sufficient for me (II Corinthians 12:9). It wasn't about being lovable; it was about remembering what God has said about me.

What is God speaking to you?

How are you loving yourself well?

Loving yourself well has everything to do with being in alignment with Christ and less about how you perform in your roles. Perfection isn't a requirement. You love yourself and others because of God's grace and love for you. Loving yourself well is a demonstration of gratitude towards the work and intentionality God put into creating you.

As a mom, loving yourself means caring for your physical and emotional health so you can pour into what is assigned to you in a healthy way. Loving yourself well is not giving in to the voice of perfectionism and procrastination but leaning into being patient with yourself and others.

Lord,

Love is a very important part of my life.
Help me to know how to love and be
loved by others. I am alive because of
Your love for me and I thank you for the
people You have placed in my life.

Amen

How can I be a better
steward of love?

PATIENCE IS KEY

But if we hope for what we do not see,
we wait for it with patience.

Romans 8:25 ESV

When I first became a mother at 19, I was young and full of dreams for my future. As years went by and I faced the challenges of being a single mother, those dreams started to feel out of reach. I was frustrated and confused about how to balance my desire to grow with my professional goals and take care of my child. I wanted to marry but how is that possible to try to date with a child?

Come along with me to the summer of 2000 my sister challenged me to try something new and take salsa lessons with her. I never had been exposed to Latin music, but as a music lover and someone who loved to dance, I gave salsa lessons a shot.

That pause I took with my sister to learn about a new culture and hobby provided me the needed time to pause in order to reflect on what I could've missed out on in life and helped to broaden my perspective on how God could show up in my life.

Patience is a beautiful attribute but it is often misunderstood. Patience is the foundation that allows you to experience and appreciate all that God has for you. Have you ever heard someone say there is a "doing while waiting?" Whether you are working towards a goal or waiting for a prayer, patience is required to live life well and maintain and express gratitude. It's the key to unlocking the full potential of our lives and our dreams. According to Galatians 6:9 ESV ,"And let us not grow weary of doing good, for in due season we will reap, if we do not give up."

How does patience play a role in your personal and professional goals? As I reflect on my journey as a mother and a professional, I realize that my patience has been the most important ingredient in my success. It has allowed me to appreciate the small unique moments and to trust that God has a plan for me. I recently stepped into the entrepreneurial space and obtained my first management position. The 19 year old me and even at 30 something I would have thought that 50 is kind of late to get started. What I know for sure is that I am right where I am supposed to be. I fully embrace the processes I experience because I understand the value in waiting and being patient with myself and others.

If you're frustrated and confused about how to balance your dreams with your responsibilities, take a step back and remember that patience is the key.

Lord,

Help me find an accountability partner.
Reveal someone to me who is safe and
helps me feel comfortable sharing when I
don't feel strong in my waiting.

Amen

How do I practice patience in my life?

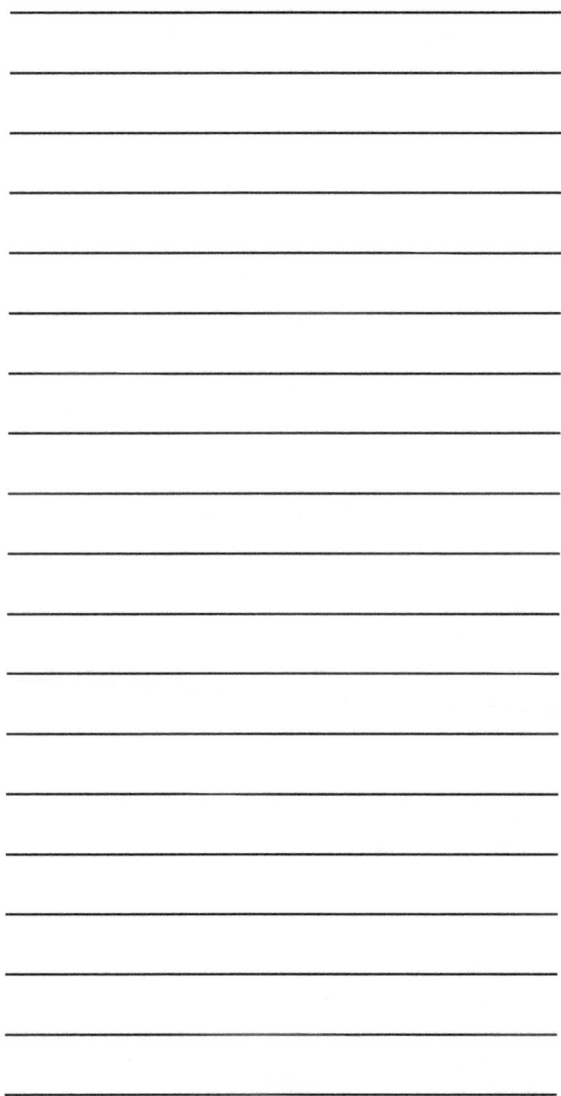

TIME TO CONNECT

" And let us consider how to stir up one another to love and good works, not neglecting to meet together, as is the habit of some, but encouraging one another, and all the more as you see the Day drawing near. "

Hebrews 10:24-25

Have you ever felt so content in life that you asked yourself, "What more could I possibly need?" That is how I felt until one weekend on my way to meet a mentor for dinner. The shopping area was busy and as I walked from my car to the restaurant, I saw people connecting. I can't explain what happened, but I started to think about my own relationships and connections. I'm busy and can easily find an excuse not to make connections because of my schedule.

Staying connected in a real way takes work and vulnerability that most of us rarely engage in while gathering with others. I began to ask myself, "Am I really taking care of my relationships?" and my answer was a sobering "No!!"

I have access to reciprocal relationships filled with honesty, humor, insight, and friendship, but I was starting to question the level of care I gave to those relationships. This has always been a struggle for me. I need to make more of an effort to have coffee with a friend or drop by to visit a loved one I haven't visited outside of a holiday.

If you have brief and obligatory contact with others is that really connecting? And is there a reciprocal pouring each other? Take a moment to think about the relationships that could use time and attention. Are cups overflowing?

Lord,

I know You created me to connect with others and live in a community. If I have not been taking care of my relationships, show me what to do to make real connections with others.

Amen

Have I been taking care of my relationships and connecting outside of a crisis or life event?

TAKE A STEP BACK

*"For no one ever hated his own flesh, but
nourishes and cherishes it, just as Christ
does the church,"*

Ephesians 5:29 (ESV)

Being a working mom is not easy. We
juggle multiple responsibilities, at home
and in the workplace, and it can be easy to
neglect self-care. I know this all too well, as
I recently experienced an injury that forced
me to take a step back and reevaluate my
priorities.

A month before I turned 49 I had a bad
fall at work. A pain shot through my body
unlike anything I had ever felt before. I
thought it was a bad ankle sprain and hoped
to be back to normal in no time. As it
turned out, I broke a bone in my foot and

tore a major ligament, requiring surgery. It was an inconvenience because I was getting back into the swing working at a local food bank post-pandemic, and being an entrepreneur.

I was becoming frustrated being out of commission for my family but had nothing else I could do but reflect and spend some much needed one-on-one time with the Lord. It's interesting how having to sit with myself made space for me to look at what makes me happy and where I feel unfulfilled.

My pondering led me to realize I truly desire joy that can be felt and experienced by me and those around me no matter the circumstances. Galatians 5:22-23 says, "But the fruit of the Spirit is love, joy, peace, forbearance, kindness, goodness, faithfulness, gentleness and self-control. Against such things there is no law."

I began to search for a therapist to assist me in learning how to express joy and not allow life's triggers to impact me the way they had previously. In this next season of life and on my healing journey towards joy, I will boldly embrace both the destination and the mindset, living them out fully.

I have seen witnessed many women who struggle to love and care for their bodies with a joyful "get to" spirit, and I feared I was heading down the same path.

Here is what I learned: it is important to strive to cultivate joy in your life, not just for yourself, but for the sake of the people around you. It's not always easy, but it's always worth it.

When you take care of yourself, you are better equipped to handle the demands of motherhood and work life. Live and protect JOY in your life the same way we strive to protect our peace.

Lord,

Forgive me for not taking time to appreciate all the blessings great and small you have provided to me. Create in me a renewed mind and fresh opportunities daily to find, walk, and honor the joyful moments in my day.

Amen

Am I taking care of myself?

LOVING THE UNLOVABLE

"Above all, keep loving one another earnestly,
since love covers a multitude of sins."

1 Peter 4:8

At one time I felt frustrated. I wanted to get away from everyone and everything because I was feeling unappreciated and unheard which led to me feeling unloved. Have you ever felt like this? I wondered, "How could God ever love someone like me when I feel that the people in my life can't love me the way I need?"

I have struggled many days in loving myself, family, and friends the way I should. It is hard to pour from an empty cup. I have learned to confess and recognize my problematic ways of thinking specifically with shame and judgement. Self- awareness about my thought life happened when I began to reach out to speak with a professional. The day I sought counsel from my therapist was the day one of many to come when I began to unpack the root of my "stinkin' thinkin'."

As a teen, I went with my mother to visit the sick and shut in. This wasn't something I enjoyed as a teen but rather I attended out of duty and if I am honest to be close with my mom. Although I wasn't ecstatic about going God saw fit to bless me by words from someone while at the visit. The brother, an older gentleman, of the older woman we were visiting sat with me briefly noticing that I was sulking and tasked me did I know that I was the apple of God's eye? And looked at him confused and muttered "no". At the time, I didn't realize it was actually in scripture and I didn't know why he was saying that to me, but I never forgot what he said. God used the man to express His love for me. Over the years, God has not only provided tangible resources to myself and my family, but He has provided peace and perspective during difficult seasons.

The word of God is a great place to begin to investigate how God loves you and how you should express and demonstrate his love to others even those who may seem unlovable. God instructs and commands us to love one another, John 13: 34-35 and 1 Corinthians 16:14. He doesn't say love those who believe like you, speak like you, or only those in your community but to love the way He loves.

Lord,

Renew my mind daily and transform my thought process. Lead me to a change in how I love myself, how I love others, how I love You. Although I am a work in progress, I will be mindful of how the Holy Spirit is operating within me.

This formerly unlovable woman is becoming a person who allows You to love me so that I can pour that love onto myself and others.

Amen

Will I trust God enough to let Him love on me?

BLOOD IN YOUR MOUTH

Don't use foul or abusive language. Let everything you say be good and helpful, so that your words will be an encouragement to those who hear them.

Ephesians 4:29 (NLT)

I wrote the title of this chapter after becoming frustrated with my family. I quickly realized that this statement has a profound meaning. You know the typical social media, electronic rant everyone goes on, I was having one of those moments. Then I felt a nudging from the Holy Spirit from Proverbs 18:21, "Life and Death are in the power of the tongue." I am going to take creative license and say that it made me think of my mouth being the cross that Christ hung on so that I could have life.

Then the phrase Blood in my mouth took on a completely different meaning to me. It wasn't a powerless, stuffing of feelings or emotions during conflict; it has become a reminder that the symbolic blood in my mouth is my sacrifice for my fellow man to make sure my word did not speak of death and harm but life and hope.

I have been told how I have the gift of influence and that people listen when I speak, but I never really thought much about the weight of those words until that very second. My words can be damaging to individuals, neighborhoods, countries, and communities. My words can lead to spiritual, emotional, and finally physical death to myself and the receiver, or I could choose words that were life giving and sustaining to the health of people and my community. Today, I choose to be intentional with my words and speak life and practice holding my responses until prayerfully listening for God's guidance.

Holding your tongue and having a thoughtful response brings about the results God is pleased with. There is an immense value in holding your tongue until you've had time to process your emotions and thoughts. Remember you are your brother's and sister's keeper and that doesn't just mean in action that means in words as well.

My relationships with my children, husband, siblings, and parents have all improved over the years as I learned to speak the truth in love Ephesians 4:15. Growing as a leader in the workplace and community has been greatly improved by learning to be intentional and understanding the symbolic meaning of having blood in your mouth. It's a sacrificial gesture made in love as child of God. I ask myself, "What is the impact going to be? What is the purpose?"

Lord,

Do I have blood in my mouth? I know
that Proverbs 16:24 says *"Kind words are
like honey—sweet to the soul and healthy for the
body (NLT)."* Help me choose my words
to build people, nations and bring about
peace. I do not want to tear your people
down.

Amen

Do I understand the power of my words?

THE TURNING POINT

"A man's gift makes room for him and brings him before the great."

Proverbs 18:16 ESV

Over a decade ago, I found myself facing a challenge that, while not directly articulated, demanded more than my expertise as a case manager. Positioned at the intersection of experience and opportunity, I recognized that the task required a blend of skills far beyond the confines of traditional case management.

With a foundation rooted in prior programming experiences, I embarked on a mission to create a family program from scratch. This initiative aimed to support families navigating the complexities of incarceration and foster meaningful moments in their reunification journey.

The endeavor wasn't an overnight success, but a gradual, intentional process that unfolded over time.

While I wasn't leading a team in the conventional sense, I found myself at the forefront of leading families we served, guiding interns seeking hands-on professional experience, and influencing colleagues and management. The essence of leadership, I discovered, lies not just in directing reporting staff but in spearheading initiatives that uplift and empower all stakeholders.

This role marked a turning point in my professional journey, revealing my innate inclination towards leadership. People began to follow my lead, including those I reported to directly. It was a revelation that crystallized my understanding of leadership as a natural inclination—one that emerges authentically when passion aligns with purpose.

Lord,

At home and in the workplace you have called me to lead in the spaces you have assigned me. Give me understanding for my ministry in that space and help me as I take steps to walk in the obedience of what you are calling me to.

Amen

Am I authentically aligned with my calling?

DISCOVERING PURPOSE IN STRUGGLE

Your eyes saw my unformed body. All the days ordained for me were written in your book before one of them came to be.

Psalms 139:16 (NIV)

It has truly been a journey seeking my purpose in God. Frustration and disappointment often set in as I tried to fit into my different roles. I tried to accomplish many things that I felt would make me feel purposeful, and important, but in reality, they only exhausted me and confused my focus on what God was trying to teach me. I wondered about who God is, His thoughts towards me, and His equipping of me to do His will.

Psalm 139:16 became one of the first scripture of impact for me. God knew I would rebel; and He provided teachable moments for me to learn from the experience. Motherhood was always His plan for me. I jumped ahead, but that never changed His thoughts toward me for a future and hope and the plan of motherhood.

Let me give you an example of how God reveals that he doesn't give up on His established plan. One day I was riding with my daughter and we were sharing a rare moment of mother-daughter time singing songs when she turned to me and said, "Mom, thanks for keeping me." Her words reverberated in my mind.

I knew my daughter's words came from God; He used her to remind me of Psalm 139:16 and Jeremiah 29:11. The latter scripture gave me peace:

"For I know the thoughts I think toward you, says the Lord, thoughts of peace and not of evil, to give you a future and a hope" (NKJV).

Part of my journey was the moment where I contemplated terminating my pregnancy. An unspoken deep secret I held onto or so I thought until God allowed my daughter to share that moment of gratitude. He saw me and he knew me.

It has taken me over 30 years of being in, and around the presence of God to finally set aside my selfish ambitions and truly trust His promises. Heroines of the Bible: Mary, Deborah, Priscilla, and so many others recorded them for us to read, recite, and remember their journeys and struggles.

He'll use you once you step out in faith. What dream have you thought impossible? What support are you seeking that you haven't received?

Lord,

Thank you for thinking of me and
establishing a hope and future for me.
Forgive me for doubting and rebelling
when Your word says that You have
established my days and promised a hope
and a future for me.

Amen.

What dream have
I thought impossible?

STRENGTH DURING TESTING

Fear not, for I am with you;
be not dismayed, for I am your God;
I will strengthen you, I will help you,
I will uphold you with my righteous right hand.

Isaiah 41:10 ESV

It can be difficult to remember how faithful, and great God is as a Father. I remember a few years ago I shared about the experience of being diagnosed with Multiple Sclerosis.

When I was first diagnosed, I was desperate for the diagnosis not to be true. See, I was a healthy child, teen, and young adult, so to have such a major diagnosis given to me was paralyzing. There was nothing anyone could say to make me feel better. No one knew the storm occurring on the inside of my body.

But God.

My three children needed me and I was recovering from the seven-year hump that married couples go through with small children. My diagnosis was given at an inconvenient time. I cried some days and went numb on other days.

One day after having a private pity party I decided to pray. God made me and I believed He knows how to fix me. I blew dust off one of the many bibles in our home and many passages stood out to me. The book of James was the most appropriate for my need that day.

Stressing, stretching, and strengthening in trials are described in the first few verses of James chapter 1. James wanted to encourage the persecuted members of the body of Christ who had been scattered throughout the regions.

Just like in the book of James' day, remain encouraged during your tests and trials. I can guarantee they are temporary. You're being equipped during your testing to not only grow and develop personally but to have an impact on the lives of others.

Lord,

I can confidently say You will not have me lose hope. The road is challenging and it is complicated but I believe Your promises. I know You will work things out for my good (Romans 8:28)

Amen

Where is my faith?

Affirmations

- I am fearfully and wonderfully made; chosen for the unique role I play in my family and community.
- I align my heart and mind with God's purpose for my life, trusting His timing and plan.
- In motherhood, I am a reflection of God's nurturing love, and I find clarity and strength in Him.
- I walk in purpose daily, embracing wisdom, grace, and peace provided by God for me.
- I am equipped to lead my family with love, patience, and divine guidance.
- God has entrusted me with the gifts of motherhood and leadership, and I honor that calling with faith.
- My clarity comes from leaning on God's wisdom, even when the path isn't clear.
- I find purpose in every season, knowing that God is refining and shaping me through each experience.

- I release the need for perfection and embrace God's grace for me today.
- I trust that God is aligning my steps with His greater purpose for my family and me.
- I am enough, just as I am, empowered to grow, learn, and thrive in every role God has given me.
- Through prayer and reflection, I find clarity in God's will for my life as a mother and leader.

Reflection Questions

- How have I witnessed God's hand guiding me in my journey of motherhood and leadership?

- In what areas of my life do I need to release control and trust God's plan more fully?

- How can I make space for God to reveal clarity and purpose in the midst of my busy daily life?

- What moments of motherhood have brought me a great sense of alignment with my God-given purpose?

- Where have I experienced a shift in my identity, and how is God calling me to embrace my new season?

- What obstacles in my life are preventing me from seeing the clarity God is offering me?

- What do I need to be loved well?

ABOUT THE AUTHOR

Dionna Rojas Orta is passionate about empowering individuals and organizations to achieve their goals and overcome their challenges. She is a certified Purpose Coach and a Master Life Coach.

Dionna has received multiple honors and awards for her leadership and mentorship, such as the Onyx Woman Emerging Leader Award, the Women of Excellence Award, and the Mentor of the Year Award. She is proficient in group facilitation, reflective listening, and workshop facilitation.

Dionna is committed to making a positive impact in her community of Pittsburgh, Pennsylvania, and beyond. She is the proud parent of three children and a loving GiGi.

STAY CONNECTED

Treasure You

🌐 DionnaRojas.com
✉ dionnarojas@gmail.com